*Presented to Dear Krishna on his Second Birthday!*

*From Aja and Aii*

*June 2, 2009*

# THE ULTIMATE

## TODDLER

### COLLECTION

## Toddler's First Memory Book

**Twin Sisters Productions, LLC**

4710 Hudson Drive Stow, OH 44224 USA

www.twinsisters.com   1-800-248-TWIN (8946)

TW1052CD   ISBN−13/EAN:978-159922-337-7

# Special Day

Today you . . . _____

_____

Date: _____

# Playtime

# So Silly

You are so silly when you . . . _____

_____

_____

_____

_____

# It's Silly Time

It's not time to be quiet. No, not at all.
It's not time to be still. Let's have a ball!
It's not time to relax or sit and wait,
for it's time to be silly and that's what I want to be.

Because it's silly, silly, silly, silly, silly, silly time.
I'm feeling all giggly-wiggly, funny, and fine.
It's fun to be silly. That's what I want to do.
Be silly, silly, silly. Won't you be silly, too?

It's not time to rest in a quiet place.
It's not time for bed. Come on, let's race!
It's not time to whisper or go to sleep,
for it's time to be silly and that's what I want to be.

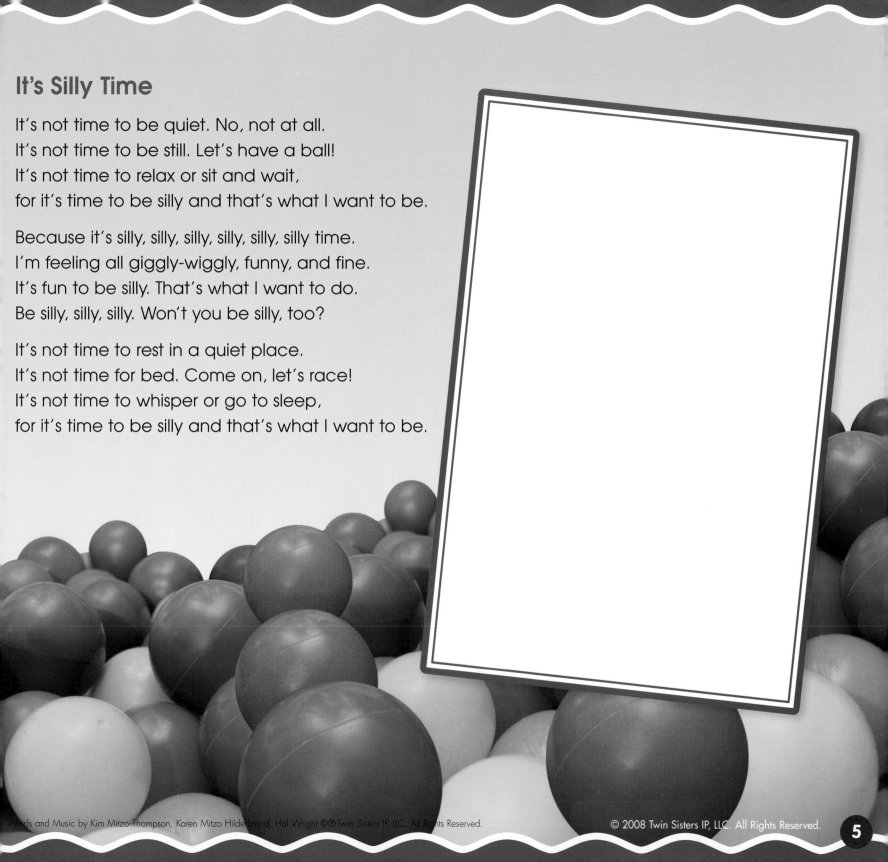

# My Bathtime Fun

## It's Bathtime

Off with the clothes,
Everybody knows
It's bathtime! Bathtime!
Into the tub,
I see lots of mud!
It's bathtime! Bathtime!

Off with the clothes,
You dirty thing!
Off with the clothes,
Is what I'll sing!
Into the tub,
You really have to scrub,
For it is bathtime.

For it is bathtime,
You know a little rub a dub.
Bathtime!
Come on and get into that tub.
For it is bathtime!
It's time to get nice and clean.
Time to scrub your neck and your knees,
And everywhere in between!
For it is bathtime!

## Get Wet

A little water on my nose.
A little water on my knees.
A little water on my chin.
It's like swimmin' in the sea.

A little water on my hands.
A little water on my feet.
A little water on my belly.
Come on, get wet with me!

Chorus
I'm singin' get wet—
The "Get Wet" song
I'm singin' get wet—
Come on and join along
I'm singin' get wet—
Cause it's time to have fun
Get wet, get wet, get wet!
It's all happenin' in the tub!

Words and Music by Kim Mitzo Thompson, Karen Mitzo Hilderbrand, Hal Wright

## Mozart's Lullaby

Sleep, little one, go to sleep.
So peaceful the birds and the sheep.
Quiet are meadows and trees,
Even the buzz of the bees,
The silvery moonbeams so bright,
Down through the window give light.
O'er you the moonbeams will creep,
Sleep, little one, go to sleep.
Good night.
Good night.

## It's Night-Night Time

It's night-night time, night-night time,
Lay your head on me.
It's night-night time, night-night time
Time to go to sleep.
I'll sing to you and hold you close.
It's night-night time, night-night time.
Time to go to sleep.

It's night-night time, night-night time,
In your crib you go.
It's night-night time, night-night time
Mommy loves you so.
I'll sing to you while you close your eyes.
It's night-night time, night-night time.
Mommy loves you so.

## It's Time For Bed

It's time for bed, time for bed.
Time to get ready for bed.
Put on your PJ's and brush your teeth.
Kisses and hugs, come snuggle with me.
It's time for bed, time for bed.
Now let's go to sleep.

Words and Music by Kim Mitzo Thompson, Karen Mitzo Hilderbrand, Hal Wright
©℗ Twin Sisters IP, LLC. All Rights Reserved.

# I Love Watching You Sleep

I thank. . .

# My _____ Birthday

# My Guests

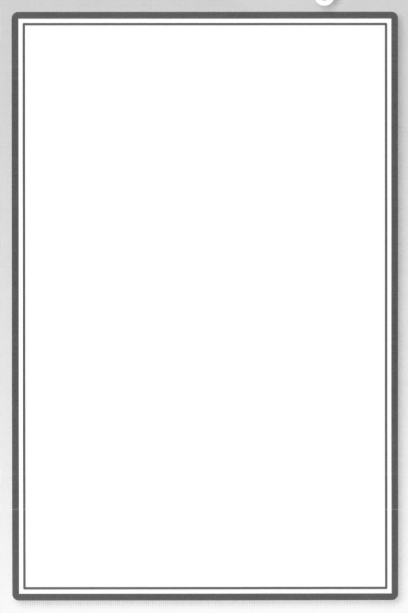

The best part of the day was _____

_____

Date: _____

# All About Me

### If You're Happy and You Know It

If you're happy and you know it, clap your hands.
If you're happy and you know it, clap your hands.
If you're happy and you know it then your
    face will surely show it.
If you're happy and you know it, clap your hands.

If you're happy and you know it, stomp your feet.
If you're happy and you know it, stomp your feet.
If you're happy and you know it then your
    face will surely show it.
If you're happy and you know it, stomp your feet.

If you're happy and you know it, shout Hooray.
If you're happy and you know it, shout Hooray.
If you're happy and you know it then your
    face will surely show it.
If you're happy and you know it, shout Hooray.

If you're happy and you know it, do all three....
If you're happy and you know it, do all three....
If you're happy and you know it then your
    face will surely show it.
If you're happy and you know it, do all three....

Words and Music by Kim Mitzo Thompson, Karen Mitzo Hilderbrand, Hal Wright ©℗ Twin Sisters IP, LLC. All Rights Reserved.

# My Friends

# At the Park

# So Big

I am _____ old

and way too cute

# Fun Things to Do

## Action Story

Use your imagination to help your child become a part of his favorite story. Act out the story. Make noises each time an animal character is mentioned. Do a movement whenever a key word is said.

## King or Queen For A Day

Cut construction paper to look like a crown. Decorate it with markers, crayons, paint, stickers, sequins, and jewels. Fit the crown to your preschooler's head and staple, glue, or tape the ends together. Declare your preschooler "King" or "Queen" for the day.

## Leaping Lily Pads

Toss socks, fabric scraps, pillows or cushions around the room—these are the lily pads. Throw a beanbag into the middle and see if your child can hop from lily pad to lily pad, pick up the beanbag, and make her way back to the beginning.

## My Recipes

Ask your young chef how to prepare a favorite meal or dessert. Write down word for word the recipe. "Thaw out the chicken for sixteen days, grease the pan with peanut butter, and cook for 36 hours!" For more fun, make a cookbook and let your young chef share the recipes with other family members.

## Walk In the Rain

Enjoy a long walk together during the next gentle rain. Splash in the puddles or try to catch raindrops on your tongue.

## Tissue Trail

Unroll a roll of bathroom tissue throughout the house—under the kitchen table, over the couch, around the chair, up the stairs. Have your toddler follow the trail to find a surprise!

## Water Race

Find a running creek, stream, or even a lake. Determine start and finish lines, then experiment to see what objects float faster from start to finish. Use sticks, twigs, leaves, or plastic float toys.

## Cloud Watching

In the backyard or at a quiet park, lie down on the grass together and look at the clouds. Talk about the shapes you see or make up stories.

## Night Hike

A walk around the neighborhood or a local park after dark doesn't need to be scary. Use flashlights to light the path, but stop occasionally to look into the trees. Turn off the flashlights, too, and look up at the sky.

## Super Hero

Make a super-hero costume out of household items —bath or kitchen towels, clothespins, aluminum foil, plastic containers for shields, etc. Make up stories about the new super hero's abilities!

## Land of Make-Believe

Give your child a real key or one made out of cardboard. Say, "This key opens the door to the land of make-believe!" Pretend to open the door together. Ask questions that require your child to imagine. "What do you see? What's happening? Who is waiting for us?"

## Hair Stylist

Let your toddler pretend to style your hair using brushes, barrettes, hair ties, and headbands. Use a handheld mirror to show you the result. Then return the favor!

# Look At Me Now

## Let's Play Make-Believe

Isn't it fun to pretend and play?
To be an astronaut in outer space?
Or a ballerina, or a famous movie star?
Playing a really loud guitar.
You can be anything you want to be.
Let's play make-believe!

Chorus
Make-believe! Use your imagination.
Make-believe! Just add some concentration.
Make-believe! No need for any instruction.
Make-believe! Put on a grand production!
Make-believe!

Isn't it fun to pretend and play?
To be a weather person on a rainy day?
Or a famous chef, or a beautiful bride?
Or a very friendly tour guide?
You can be anything you want to be.
Let's play make-believe!

Chorus
Be a baseball player, or work at the zoo.
Drive a taxicab down Fifth Avenue.
Own your own restaurant or small café.
You can do anything when you play!

# I Like To...

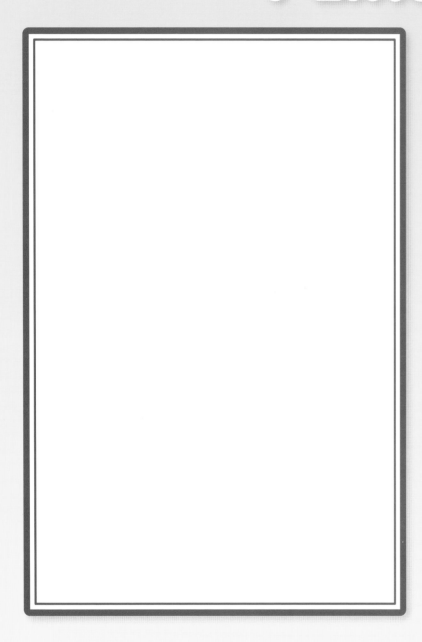 

# People Who Love Me

# I Can Wiggle

I can wiggle my fingers.
I can wiggle my toes.
I can wiggle my elbows.
And even my nose.
I can wiggle my ankles.
I can wiggle my knees.
I can wiggle, wiggle,
Wiggle every part of me.

I can wiggle, wiggle, wiggle, wiggle, wiggle, wiggle;
I can wiggle all of me.
I can jiggle, jiggle, jiggle, jiggle, jiggle, jiggle;
Just take a look at me.
I can shimmy. I can squirm.
I can look just like a worm.
I can wiggle, wiggle, wiggle, wiggle, wiggle, wiggle;
I'm a wiggle worm!

Watch me wiggle my fingers.
Watch me wiggle my toes.
Watch me wiggle my elbows.
And even my nose.
Watch me wiggle my ankles.
Watch me wiggle my knees.
Watch me wiggle, wiggle, wiggle every part of me.

# I Can Do It!

I can do it, do it, do it, do it,
Do it by myself.
I can do it, do it, do it, do it,
Do it without your help.

I can brush my teeth.
I can comb my hair.
I can clean my room.
And hug my teddy bear.
With my PJ's on,
And my toys away,
And a kiss goodnight,
In my bed I'll stay.

Goodnight!

Words and Music by Kim Mitzo Thompson, Karen Mitzo Hilderbrand, Hal Wright ©℗ Twin Sisters IP, LLC. All Rights Reserved.

# I Can...

# Look! I Drew These Pictures

Date: _____

# My First Haircut

# Funny Faces

# Christmas Memories

# My Favorite Pictures

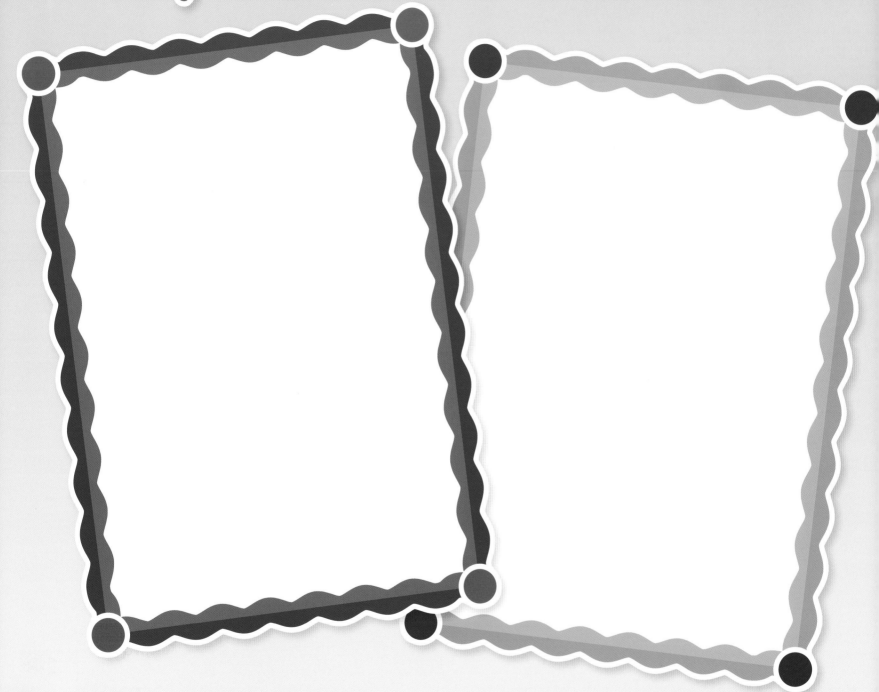

My days are fun. I spend
most of the time . . .

I laugh when . . .

_____

_____

_____

_____

_____

_____

# Facts About Me

I am _____ old.

I weigh _____ .

I am _____ tall.

My eyes are _____ .

My hair is _____ .

My best friend is _____ .

Love you so

too much fun

on
the
go

Funny
Face

ready to play

too
cute

Toddlers
Rock

# My Family

# My Handprints

Left

# Right

# I am _____ old

I like to. . .

_____

_____

_____

_____

_____

_____

_____

_____

_____

_____

_____

_____

_____

I like to. . .

_____

_____

_____

_____

# So Big

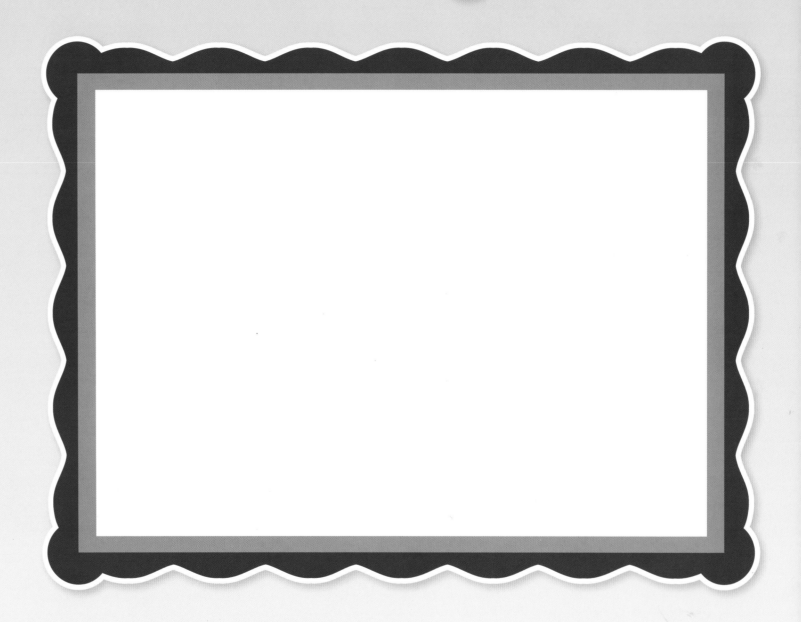

# So Loved

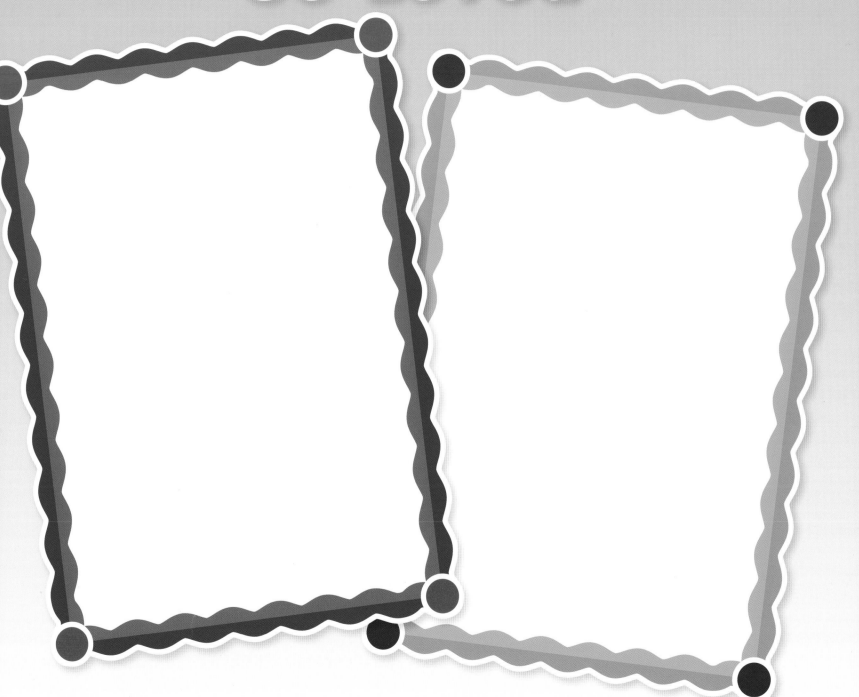

# I'm All Faces!

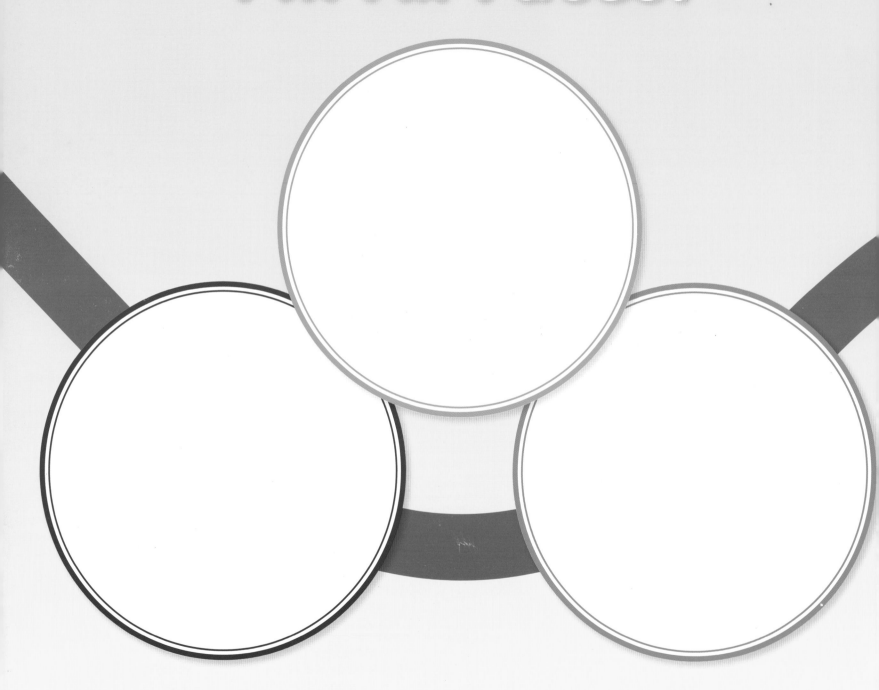